The Travel Bible for Rookies

An Insider's Guide to Successful Travel

Table of Contents

Introduction:

Meet the Travel Geek

Hi readers, and welcome to this journey. Let me quickly introduce myself, and then let's jump right into the fascinating world of travel.

I did my apprenticeship in a travel agency and have worked in the industry for many, many years. As a passionate traveler myself, I definitely can give you the best tips on how to make your trip a most unforgettable experience. I figured out even today, when all the information seems so easy to get, that many travel beginners get stuck. They have many questions or only confidently travel when they trust the information. I want to give you a book that takes you behind the curtain of a huge industry with all its weird and sometimes illogical ways.

I was born and raised in Switzerland in the middle of Europe, but in fact, it's not Europe. See, here is the first confusing part, but I will explain it later in detail. What I want to mention is that I am not based in the United States and might see things differently from readers who live there. I hope you enjoy this book and wherever it may take you, have safe travels and unforgettable moments.

Chapter 1:

How Traveling Changed

Us

In the old days, it was very complicated to travel somewhere. It took a lot of time and a lot of money to travel from point A to point B. For that reason, most people mostly stayed near home and never adventured over the next hill because it felt far away. Then the big change started with the steam trains, then the first cars, buses, and at the end, air travel was born. From that moment on, everything seemed possible. Two dots on the map got much closer than ever before, and people realized there was so much to see in the world. Modern travel had begun and has never stopped again. People now rush into planes and fly over the Atlantic Ocean— just for a weekend. Parents visit the kids 500 miles away in a faraway city, easily reachable by train or car. All this brought a new industry to life; the travel industry was born.

The travel industry includes almost everything from hotels, airlines, cruises, car rentals, and the classic travel agency. In fact, I did my apprenticeship in a brick-and-mortar travel agency. These agencies mainly existed, and a few still exist, because travelers long ago needed an overview of products or destinations. The agent has this information and is willing to share it with the customer—for a fee, of course! Also, hotel reservations or plane tickets can be ordered through agencies. This can be pricey because the agencies know how to get the money out of your pocket for their services.

And here comes the hardest and most bittersweet fact: If you know how to travel and book all the connections, you don't need a travel agency at all. In fact, you'll get trained by me to be like a *Bachelor of Travel* and know where to find what information. So no more detours, but just pure traveling.

I would say it was around the 2000s when traveling lost its childhood and became more tricky, more time-consuming, and more annoying. The World Trade Center attack was the start of it all—is my guess. Maybe you remember the old days when it was possible to bring your loved ones to the runway. You could, in fact, be with them until they climbed into the plane. These days are sadly gone, and it seems to me that now you have to show officials your passport at least ten times. You have to remove your trousers four times because of additional security. Then you must explain to the officer that you just want to take the flight and don't have any palm trees from abroad hiding in your bags. In fact, it got very crappy at times. Airports now even insist on duty-free bags for airport purchases. Yeah, it's way more complicated.

Also, our modern smartphones and social media are a part of that complication. The whole travel industry tries to save money on staff and wants you to do the work for them. Sometimes it's not too obvious—but don't you find it strange that you—as the customer, now have the "great opportunity" to do your hotel check-in online? Or how do you explain that you now have to tag your bag at the airport and drop it off yourself? All these are small puzzle parts of the industry—with a marketing twist. They say, "Hey, how amazing! We now allow you to drop your 10-pound bag by yourself at the check-in. But we have a person there who likes to watch you do it. I guess that person stays in a good mood the whole day.

Okay, enough of the negative thoughts. How can you turn it to your advantage? Know how to play the game and what to avoid, and you still can save tons of money and beat them using their own weapons. I'll show you all the steps, and I promise you that you will see the world of travel with smart new eyes—not like the tourist who reserves an overpriced $55 freeway motel.

So are you ready? Then let's start with the most important things.

Chapter 2:

How to Start and Plan Your

Journey

It sounds stupid, but first, you need to know where you're traveling to. It just doesn't make sense to search a city map for Madrid when you're, in fact, traveling to Sweden. So the first thing is to get to know your environment. What do I mean by that? Know the main facts about your destination. Here is a quick overview of my checklists for the start of a journey.

- What is the currency at the destination?

- What is the climate like? Cold, warm, or both?

- Locate a hotel that fits in with your budget but also has a good location.

- Think about ground transport—how to get from A to B.

- What documents do you need to enter the country? Passport, visa, vaccination certificates, etc.

- Insurance questions, what happens if you have an accident or need to see a doctor? How expensive is medical help at the destination?

- Language skills, not all countries speak English. Do you need a translation book or app on your phone ready, just in case?

- Safety at the destination. Is it safe to walk around? What about robberies and theft?

- Make sure you have a city map for your destination. Or at least an idea of where the main relevant tourist attractions are.

- Airport information, how long does the check-in last at the destination to return home?

- Check about the local food when you arrive. What for you might seem disgusting or bad might be the gourmet cuisine of your destination. If you're heading to Asia, find out before you travel if there is food that you definitely should avoid. This also might affect you if you have a specific allergy to some food ingredients.

- An important aspect is the tech stuff. I am talking here about all electronic devices and similar. Make sure you pack a power bank because you don't know if there are ways to recharge devices immediately. Get a second pair of headphones, as you never know if one pair will break. Believe me—they do from time to time.

- Bring your e-reader with you, fully loaded, before you leave home. Are you taking your laptop with you? Make sure to pack enough power chargers, cables, and all you need for it. In fact, a lot of countries have different power sockets from the United States, so be prepared and buy at least two for Europe, the United Kingdom, and Asia—you'll need them from time to time.

- Check your cellphone contract about roaming in foreign countries. Otherwise, you'll have a big surprise when coming back. If roaming is not included, don't forget to switch the function off on your cell phone before you leave the country. I usually do it at the gate.

All this might sound a bit over the top, but believe me—there is nothing worse than arriving somewhere and having no clue how things work. It is a thing with international trips, as all countries work in unique ways and with local habits. The more you know about specific details of your travel destination, the more you will feel safe and confident about everything, and the more you can enjoy the environment.

Just keep in mind to pre-check all these things before you start heading to the airport. Otherwise, you probably won't be able to check all preparation items off the list before the plane leaves the airport.

Chapter 3:

How to Fix a Budget

The budget for your journey is an essential part of the whole deal. I know tons of people who travel with the last dime they own and are disappointed that they haven't got money to enjoy themselves. The money issues become so stressful that they don't enjoy their time abroad. It's best to create a budget starting with expected costs.

- Travel costs: plane ticket, train ticket, car rental, hotel rooms, local transportation—these you can check ahead of your journey. Maybe also special insurance that covers you when traveling overseas. Make sure you check with your insurance company.

After you've made a budget for the definitive travel costs, you should add another budget for the everyday things you'll need at your destination. Don't cheat yourself and calculate less than you know or would like it to be. The costs are coming anyway.

- Food costs: Overcalculate them; the good thing is that you can then enjoy ice cream without sweating and recalculating every time you want one. Europe is incredibly pricey with food but so worth it. Add about 30 percent more than you expect for food. If you don't need it, great—you'll have more shopping money left.

- Shopping and gift costs: You know all your relatives want something from faraway countries, right? So make sure you calculate that too. And hey, you want to go shopping too, for sure!

- Also include a small amount for *unexpected situations.* That can be the extra fees at an airport for additional bags and special fees or entry payments for museums, etc.

I think a budget is one of the major steps for your travel. You might think that the more money you have, the more options you have. This is true sometimes, but not always. Traveling smart these days can save you hundreds of dollars without knowing it. As a reminder, the further your journey is in the future, the more possibility there is to save money and choose the best option for your plans. When you do your calculations, I strongly suggest keeping a credit card in mind. Your credit card should not be used to spend more money on things that are not needed, but it gives you safety. For example, if you need to go to a hospital in an emergency, or a flight gets canceled, and you need to book another flight, which is more expensive than you expected. Also, a credit card sometimes offers insurance for cancellation fees for hotels or flights. Check with your card provider about what is covered and what is not. Another thing to remember is that you often need a credit card to get reservations for cars, flights, or hotel rooms. The reason is that it proves that you are a customer with the money to book something and can afford to pay for it.

The last point is that several credit cards offer special programs for travelers who often fly with the same airlines or use the same hotel chains. Also, more and more car rentals provide special offers for credit card owners. If you are considering getting a new credit card, you should get one that offers the most value. That means searching for a card that gives you *cash back* on flights. Keep in mind to choose a big network, because it gives more chances to collect a bonus. If only one airline has a bonus program, the chances are that you won't use it as much, as you are unlikely to travel to destinations served by smaller airlines. The same goes for hotel chains and car rentals. Always carefully search where you get a good variety of rewards, which pushes up the chances of a cheaper flight or hotel room.

The travel industry always wants to make money on its own, of course! But if you're clever, that is no reason to stay home or travel far away. I'll show you how to do all that. Personally, I do my budget with my laptop. The reason is that I'll usually take the computer with me to adjust my budget during the trip, and I keep a clear overview, like a bookkeeper. In the end, you will be more relaxed when you travel and with the knowledge that you have everything under control.

Chapter 4:

How to Find the Smoothest and Cheapest Way From A to B

A big mystery in the travel industry is how to get from A to B cheaply. This includes all kinds of transport, from planes, buses, trains, ships, and car rentals. To understand the *main things* about prices, let's dig into details. Why are prices expensive or cheap? It's simple. If a plane, for example, would have to fly half empty because it's a Tuesday afternoon flight when not many people fly, then the airlines have to lower the prices to ensure a few more people book that flight. It's always a matter of demand. And this works for all transport, no matter what. Another thing is that prices can be lower if you're willing to layover instead of heading directly to your destination. This is often the case with trains, planes, and buses. So if you know where you want to go, I would follow the following steps:

Decide When You Wish to Travel

Let's do an example of a fictional journey. Let's say we're traveling from New York to Paris in France. We've fixed a budget and are checking for cheap opportunities. So how do we start? If you have a business trip, you'll have no choice but to travel to fit in with the dates needed in Paris. If you're a private traveler, then things look different. First, let's think about the destination as itself. Paris lies in Europe, which means the winters are cold, gray, and humid. Not a perfect time to visit the city of love. On the other hand, during the winter, the prices can get cheap and affordable. So we have to think about where our priorities are. Okay, we're going cheap now!

Search For Flights

Search for flights from New York to Paris, and keep in mind that New York and Paris have more than one airport. Start with the airline of the country you want to visit. In our example, this would be Air France. Check the option for pricing and be flexible as possible. Then do another search for flights from New York to Paris, this time via another hub. London is, for example, close to Europe and is a huge destination. Maybe it's worth flying to London's Heathrow Airport instead of flying direct to Paris. A travel secret these days is flying in small airplanes like an Airbus A321LG via Ireland, so also keep this in mind.

Keep Transfer Times in Mind

If you have to travel via an airport in Europe in winter, my tip is to make sure you have enough time to change planes and do the transfer. If it's icy, snowy, cold, and gray, many airports in Europe have bigger delays or pretty often cancel flights.

Now you should have an idea of how to move smoothly and cheaply from A to B.

From my own experience, I found the weirdest way of traveling was also the coolest and sometimes even the cheapest. For example, once, I wanted to visit Miami, but I lived in Europe. So, I suspected cruise liners would move their ships from Europe to the States after the fall. And it really was the case. I took a five-day cruise from Barcelona to reach Miami, with stops in the Azores and Bermuda. I felt relaxed with a balcony stateroom, and it only cost $499 for the trip, including food and entertainment. The flights were much more expensive. So you see, always think outside the box—it can be worth it.

I know that Americans especially try to travel around the world in four days, and they return feeling as though they haven't had a relaxing vacation. But keep in mind the difference between traveling and rushing through countries. Traveling is understanding cultures and having a glass of red wine on the Spanish Steps in Rome and talking to people, and getting a feel for the destination. Rushing is when travelers are two hours in Vienna and run then to another city on their to-do list.

This is not traveling—this is a home run. You'll return back home with only pictures on your camera but no travel soul inside your heart.

I always think of planning a journey as a game. These days it's easy to find a map on your computer and check out your destination in detail. Think about all the funny options you would have to get there. Keep open-minded and also check out other travel blogs. Often you don't have to search too long, as other people have discovered some destinations and you would just have to copy them. The more creativity you have, the more money you save. I've had this experience hundreds of times and still have to smile when it works again.

One last thing I want to point out comes with a small warning. Especially after the pandemic, you'll find out that airlines push their sales and try to tell you that they are the cheapest, best, and most efficient. Be careful with these ads. Ask yourself, is it really a good price? And is the price they publish the real price you will have to pay? Often their advertisements claim: "*Woo Hoo!* $299 for a flight to no man's land." And if you look closer, you'll find out, *aha*, they charge $199 for the baggage, $34 for security tax, and $60 for a seat reservation. And then ask yourself, is it still cheap? Or do others offer lower prices, including all the services? So you'll see, it's like a bazaar, and you're the customer who strolls through the shops. But I can guarantee you, after a while, you'll become an expert and get a feeling for prices and sales tactics, and I hope this book will help you not fall into these traps.

Chapter 5:

A Word About Hotels and How They Work and Get Your Money

Hotels have existed for thousands of years, and they all work in a similar way: Make the client happy with good hospitality and try to make as much money out of him as possible with side hustles. In the old days, all hotels were independent. This meant that every hotel worked by itself and was on the lookout to find better ways of getting guests into their establishments.

After traveling became more popular and tourists traveled further, hotel chains came into the picture. The whole hotel industry benefited from this phenomenon because, at any stage, the customer knows what to expect from the hotel. If you pick out a random hotel chain and book a room in Tahiti and one in Chicago, you'll find that they have similar, if not exact, copies of the room. This is the aim of owners of hotel chains. They usually give investors some kind of franchise business and tell them exactly what the hotel should look like, how the rooms are designed, and what the guest can expect from it. Also, the price has to be in the same range. The pricing is a way to gain an advantage as a traveler. You have to think countywide to understand what I mean. Let's pretend you're the owner of the 5-star luxury hotel chain "Golden Palace." You have right now two hotels under this brand, one in Rome and one in Bangkok. Now tell me, which one is cheaper? You'll probably say the one in Bangkok, which might be correct from your point of view. But if you're a Thai living in Thailand and look up hotel prices in Bangkok, it will feel costly. The thing is that every country has expenses like hotel staff payments, taxes, and other things, and depending on the country, they are higher or lower. And with all those differences, it happens that the same luxury hotel is much cheaper in some cities than in others.

Let's talk quickly about breakfast in hotels. Usually, they are pretty expensive for the amount of breakfast you get. Sometimes you might be lucky, and the buffet is amazing, but from my experience of over 35 years of travel, the breakfast is usually way too expensive. But why is this? It's easily explained; the hotel knows you're lazy and want your breakfast coffee without delay or even before wandering around the neighborhood. And that's why, almost every time, they get you to pay for the overpriced breakfast. To save money, you can check in advance, while relaxing at home, what kind of restaurants are in the area. You will find they are mostly only a few steps down the road and will cost you 50 percent less than the hotel breakfast. The same thing goes for dinner, by the way. Whenever a restaurant is located within the hotel, you can expect it to be more expensive than somewhere out on the street. It has even happened to me. I could have spent less walking from the hotel to my destination; instead, I took my lazy butt to the hotel's front door and took a cab.

I can promise you that if you're traveling a lot, you get a feeling about which hotel chains are made for you. And you want to stay with them wherever you travel. In such cases, getting a membership card from a particular hotel chain definitely makes sense. Usually, they come for free and allow you to collect points for your stayovers. If you have saved enough points, the hotel will spoil you with a room upgrade into a higher category or a complimentary breakfast, for example.

Hotel member cards only make sense if you're sure that the points don't expire and if the member card contains collecting options for all hotels within the same franchise organization. So it's definitely worth it, if you travel a lot, to find out if the place you love to stay is part of a hotel chain that offers something like that. Don't get confused, the hotel can have different names, but the main brand stays the same. Often you find this information somewhere small on the hotel page itself.

A small tip here from my end is also to check the hotel prices on their direct page and compare them with other booking platforms. You'll be surprised that you often get a better price on the hotel page directly because, of course, the hotel doesn't have to pay the online platform a fee for getting you into their rooms.

Chapter 6:

A Word About Flights and

Planes

The world of planes, flights, and airports could be a book in itself. No matter if you like flying or hate it, there is the magic behind these perfectly timed logistics and perfectionism around the globe. As a beginner, you may need clarification on a few points, which I can help you with. The most important thing first is to calm the *fear of checking in*. If you bought your plane ticket, you just have to do this:

- Print out your flight ticket. It's better to have it somewhere in paper format. After all, you may not be able to access your cellphone at the airport because you have no Wi-Fi or similar issues. If you have it on paper, there is no worry at all, and you have peace of mind.

- When you arrive at the airport, find out at what terminal your flight departs from, and proceed there.

- You'll find a *check-in* sign somewhere, and it could be the old-fashioned way with someone checking in your bags and putting the baggage claim tags on them, or you have to do it via a computer terminal.

- Either way, you'll need your passport number now, your boarding pass number, and sometimes your destination. The passport number is easy to find on its main page; it's marked as that. The boarding pass number is printed on your ticket and is mostly a long number with around ten digits or more. The first three digits are always for the airline in a coded form.

- If you have done all that on the computer, you'll be able to print out the baggage tag for your bag. The tag contains the ticket number, a baggage claim number, and the three-letter code of your destination. The three-letter code is used worldwide and, for example, could be ORD, which stands for Chicago O'Hare Airport.

- Attach the tag to your luggage and bring it to the drop-off area. Now you can wave goodbye to your bag and hope it arrives safely with you at your destination. You can stick the baggage claim number on your boarding pass so everything is together. You only need the claim number if your bags should get lost somewhere. This would be the reference for the bag itself.

- Now, you follow the signs to the security area with only your hand luggage. Make sure you don't have water bottles or similar with you. The security will take it away anyway. Now, this might change a bit, but after seeing hundreds of airports, I can say that the security show is always a bit different and a bit weird. You put all your belongings into a tray, including shoes and belts, and walk to the beep machine that recognizes metal stuff if you are still wearing some. Don't stress yourself out at this procedure, even though you might feel nervous, because the security personnel are usually not the type you want to have at your garden party. Keep your boarding pass and passport in your hand while heading through security. After you have done the *striptease* show, you get all your belongings, and you are ready to dress properly again. Check the tray once again in case you have forgotten something. After all this is done, you're almost there.

- Now you can check for the gate from where your plane will leave. Don't underestimate distances, especially if you're in a huge airport; it takes *weeks (or so, it seems)* to get to your gate. Also, a word about souvenirs, drinks, and food after the security: They are usually overpriced because the airport knows that there is nowhere else for you to go, so the chances are big that you are going to buy something very expensive.

- After you find your gate, you'll see tons of people hovering around the boarding table like lions waiting for food. I don't know why this always happens, but it's crazy to see. I usually am one of the last people to board the plane. Why? It's pretty simple, you're sitting in this small airplane seat for hours to travel from A to B, and to be honest, the travel will not be shorter because you're the guy heading to your plane seat first. Ground staff will wait for all others on board, too, so don't stress yourself by being first in the line. Be a pro!

In general, I think that for most people, traveling by plane is the most stressful mode of transport and the one which usually needs the most preparation before leaving home.

When you fly long haul, you'll find another not-so-charming part of flying— jet lag. Jet lag happens when the airplane changes time zones faster than your body can handle. In fact, the human body can adjust for about two hours per day time difference without any issues. But everything over that, you'll suffer from jet lag. This means that your body is in another time zone than you actually are. When you fly from Europe to the United States, for example, I bet you'll be one of the first in the queue at the coffee shop before it has even opened because you wake up pretty early and are ready for the day. After lunch, it might change, and you may get sleepy and tired in the middle of the day. Usually, the body also needs one full day to adjust to two hours of time difference. That means if there is a six-hour time difference from where you started your trip, you will need three days to feel yourself again. The thing with jet lag is that everyone has different symptoms. A few don't feel it at all, but others, like me, for example, suffer a bit more from it.

- There is no trick to take it off the list completely, but a few tips might help ensure that it will go away soon. During the flight, drink a lot of water or tea. Avoid alcoholic beverages or coffee if possible.

- When you arrive, make sure to take a walk to get your blood pumping again after many hours of sitting in a plane chair.

- Tell your body that it is now the time you actually are at; you would be amazed how a mindset can change that feeling of jet lag.

- Do some fitness exercises in the gym, which usually helps me a lot.

- Try to avoid eating heavy food when you arrive; a salad should do it, or a few fruits.

- Melatonin is available worldwide at pharmacies and helps make you sleep. It is very effective and has no real side effects.

Chapter 7:

A Word About Trains in

Europe

Okay! This topic might not be interesting for everyone
traveling around the globe. But for some, it is crucial, so
I decided to include it in the book. Traveling by train
could be one of the fastest and the most scenic ways to
get around while in Europe. When you're planning a
train journey in Europe, you have to ask yourself: Are
you traveling within one country, or do you hope to
visit others too? Depending on your answer, your
planning changes. It can get confusing because every
country has its own national train company, and all
these sell different tickets. If you know that you're
traveling a lot and to different countries, there is a
special ticket called a *rail pass* which allows you to
combine different countries on one ticket.

Night trains are becoming more popular in Europe
after a few years of stopping altogether. If you visit
major cities, it is cool to board your train after dinner,
sleep in it and arrive relaxed the following day in
another city. Prices change quickly with night trains,
depending on how fully booked the train is. You

definitely want to check if it's cheaper to fly or to take the train to your destination. Sometimes even cheap bus companies offer the same journey at an attractive price.

When you travel by train, you don't have to worry about how many bags you can carry; it doesn't matter at all. What you definitely want to do, even if it costs a few dollars more, is to reserve your seat on the train. Especially on Fridays when the trains are overcrowded, you want to have a seat reserved. You'll be sitting and relaxed while others have to stand in the aisles. With the exception of Switzerland, allow yourself enough time to change trains if needed. In Switzerland, 99 percent of the time, the trains are on schedule, so even a seven-minute change is easy. But bigger countries like Germany, for example, struggle to keep their timetable more or less on track. When you travel on EuroCity-trains, it usually has a restaurant car. Sometimes they are overpriced, and the quality of the food and drink is bad—but occasionally, you might be lucky. I always recommend that you buy your food and drinks in advance for longer train trips. You never know what's coming. If you're a speed freak, you definitely should test out some of the fast tracks in Europe. These include:

- Eurostar (the train between London and Paris goes underneath the North Sea.)

- Intercity Express (ICE) is a German high-speed train that covers a big network of cities at affordable prices.

- France's high-speed train (TGV) is definitely worth a try. This train is made for speed and long distances. If you have a chance to travel out of Paris, test it out, it's awesome, as you feel like a Formula 1 driver.

If you're more of a scenic guy than a speedster, try out the trains from north to south in Switzerland or Austria. They all go over great mountain passes with beautiful landscape scenery. Expect to plan more time, as the scenic trains are not the fastest usually because of the terrain they have to pass through. A train journey belongs to Europe—like good food, that's for sure!

Chapter 8:

A Word About Cruises

Cruises are a giant in the travel industry. Not only because there are so many ships out there, but more and more people want to spend their free time on the water. This can be on the seven seas or also on rivers around the world. For me, the fun thing about cruise traveling is that you never find a person who likes it "a little bit" There are only two groups here, those who hate it to the bone and those who love it. Thankfully I am one of those people who love being on ships. When you consider going on your first cruise, I have a few important tips that might help you find your perfect cruise. First of all, you have to decide if you want to make a river or sea trip. Personally, I prefer the sea for a simple reason—river cruise ships may have all amenities that bigger ships usually have, but it's all a bit smaller. Before you go, you might want to find out what cruise suits you. So here are a few steps to think about:

- The most difficult part is to find your perfect cruise liner. There are cruise liners that offer more fun for young people or families, and on the other hand, there are cruises that are made for a luxurious traveler. All have positive aspects; it's just important to match your needs. For example, on vacation, I don't want to plan on what time my dinner should be. So I would choose a freestyle cruise where I can decide when and what to eat.

- I would recommend a big ship with lots of variety. You ask why? Of course, there are more travelers on that ship, but the whole thing is made for more people. You get a chance to find out what you like and what's a waste of money and time. And after a week on one of the mega-ships, you'll see for yourself if you want to try smaller ships because, for example, you find that you have not used half the entertainment program. Also, prices can be very attractive on big ships because they have to fill up the ship with paying customers—when they cannot fill it up, they flood the market with cheap tickets.

- Cabins are another huge topic to discuss. There are several types of cabins. You'll have inner cabins without daylight at all. They are cheap, but to be honest, I don't want to feel like I'm traveling in a submarine or a prison. Then you have cabins with windows, which are okay-ish, but I would always go for a balcony cabin, if possible. The reason is that you can get fresh air, sit on the balcony and enjoy the sea breeze. Isn't that why you are going on a ship? Don't save too much money on the cabin; it's your vacation, after all! When you're new to cruising, start with a cabin in *midships*, which means in the middle of the ship. This is where the movement of the ship is not that intense. Anyway, pack seasick pills in your luggage, just to make sure. If you don't need them, that's absolutely fine, but at least you have an option if you do.

- *Embarkation day* is the day you finally board the ship. Get your passport ready and your cruise voucher. Normally you must be at the cruise terminal around two hours before the ship leaves. Your bags will get delivered directly to your rooms, so you don't have to worry about pushing them around the ship. A few things you should pack in your hand luggage include a change of clothing. Rooms are mostly not ready when you check in at the terminal, but maybe you want to hop in the pool, so pack all your bathing stuff for that reason. Also, sunscreen and sunglasses are highly recommended.

- At the terminal, you will also get your *room card*, which is also your card for all payments and much more. Make sure you don't lose it! Also, if you go ashore during your trip, the room card works almost like a passport: To reenter the ship, you'll need your room card. I would say that embarkation day is the most stressful day of your whole journey on the cruise. You have to remember that maybe 5,000 people have to get off the ship, and 5,000 need to get on board. Between that, they have to clean all the rooms, so it's quite hectic.

- After you settle in, the first mandatory thing is the security drill. This is for a good reason because it shows you what to do in an emergency. Normally it includes directions to the master station. There is also a map on your cabin door with details of the safety protocols. Because there are so many travelers, they split safety drills into smaller groups for instructions on how to put on life vests and so on. It will take around 20 minutes, and then you are free to do whatever you want to do.

- Food is another consideration on cruise ships. Normally the food is very good, and you can order as much as you want because the food is included in your fare. The cruise liner tries to hook travelers with upscale restaurants on board, and these cost extra—although typically not too much more. Is the fee worth it? In my opinion, most of the time, yes! Especially if you have a great steakhouse on board. Then I'm happy to pay $20 for a good meal. Drinks are another thing to keep in mind when on board.

Cruise lines can be confusing with their *drink packs* and what's included and what's not. The thing for you and your family will be to consider what to have. Ask yourself: How much do I drink? How much alcohol do I drink? Is good coffee important to me? How about a special wine? Do I drink that much wine? After so many years of cruising, I find that it is enough to buy a *soda package,* which is around $15 a day and includes soda drinks and, most of the time, beer. But of course, when you are someone who drinks more or wants to drink wine on board regularly, you should check out the prices because maybe it's worth upgrading the package.

- Shore trips organized by the cruise are mostly expensive. I will give you an example to show what I mean. I went to Cancún, and the cruise I was booked on wanted $190 to visit Tulum, a historical place not too far away. It was a day trip and was very expensive. I organized a trip by myself before my journey started at home. I paid $35 for the same trip, including lunch and drinks, and had the time of my life with the locals. So here you can see how cruise liners make money and where. Also, if you buy some merchandise t-shirts or go gambling in the ship casino, they make an extra buck out of you.

But to be fair, while normally cruises cost a great deal of money, you get a whole *ship experience*, great food, lots of entertainment, a nice cabin, and best of all, you don't have to pack and unpack your bags many times while the ship takes you to the many destinations you want to see.

River cruises are more or less the same but in smaller vessels. I can recommend, for example, a river cruise on the river Rhein in Germany and you won't be able to say anything bad about it. Just make sure to keep in mind that older travelers enjoy river cruises. Whether you choose a river or the open waters of the sea, it will always impact you at some point, and you may struggle with living with so many people in close proximity. But even on a 7,400-person ship, I've always found a cozy place to read a book, enjoy a coffee with friends, or just watch the waves go by.

Chapter 9:

A Word About Car Rentals

Worldwide

If you travel anywhere in the world, the chances are very big that you will rent a car. Most of the time, when public transport could be better or nonexistent, you definitely need a car. For those circumstances, the industry gave you car rental companies. I always recommend big international car rental companies, as you know then that they have experience and most have relatively new cars. Check different companies to get a feeling for the costs. If you rent for a more extended period, like a week or more, the cars usually are cheaper. When I rent a car, I always follow these steps:

- Find out if you need the car for a one-way trip from A to B or if you need to bring the car back to the same station where you've rented it. That sometimes changes the rental fee.

- A quick tip here on the side: If you need to rent a car from an airport, it often is worth a ride by taxi to a nearby location downtown. The prices are normally lower. This is because car rental companies know you're lazy and can charge you higher prices at the airport.

- If you found the company of your trust, ask yourself how big a car you need. Rentals often show you bigger car categories to tease you, but ask yourself, do you need an SUV if you're only driving the car for two days? Prices are higher; it may need more gas, etc. So choosing the smaller vehicle could be a good saving.

- When it comes to rental prices, I recommend checking if the rental prices come with insurance. I always take the full coverage because it might look a bit more expensive, but if something happens during your rental, it saves tons of money and a lot of trouble, believe me!

- Another thing where rental companies make money is with *car GPS*. Usually, they make you pay separately for a GPS, which should be included free in every car in the world. So if you have your own portable GPS at home, bring it and save money. Just make sure you have downloaded the actual map from the country you are traveling to.

- Check your contract to see if you have to fill up the car when you get it back or if you can leave it empty. I mention this because if you bring the car back empty and the rental station fills it up for you, they can charge you tons of extra money for something you could easily do two miles down the road for lower prices. Also, determine if the miles you drive are all included in the final price. I remember once a company told me they *just charge 10 cents every mile*. It doesn't sound that much, but believe me, in big countries like the United States, it mounts up really quickly and finally gets very expensive.

- The last crazy piece of advice I can give you is for you to ask directly for a lower price when you collect the car. I once had a case where I got a *family reduction* on a car. I put a baby basket on the back seat. I have no kids at all, but hey, it saved me $200, and so I drove through Canada with a baby basket in my back seat, always empty—well, not always empty. I found out the basket is the perfect place to store the big-size packs of chips and sweets. So you see, always ask for special prices!

Chapter 10:

Why Less Is Sometimes

More, the Fear About Not

Seeing Everything

Let's be realistic; you will never see the whole world. There is not enough time, and the other thing is, this earth is pretty big. So when you are young, of course, you think you'll see all there is to see. But what usually happens? You stress about countries you want to see, but did you really see them? For me personally, there is a difference between *going somewhere* and *traveling*. When I speak of traveling, I mean going to a place and soaking up the culture, food, and people. I know many, many tourists in my home town in Basel, Switzerland, who like to go to a destination rather than travel. They stay a few hours and rush to the next country. Often, they don't even have a clue where they are anymore. I would never do a European tour in five days, for example. Why? Because this is not traveling but stressing and not seeing anything at all. I always try to pick a place, location, or city of interest and stick to it. Why is this?

Experience after over 30 years of traveling. I have spent the best evenings of my life with locals sitting in Florence, Italy, drinking red wine and chatting endlessly. For me, this is what travel means.

So, if you also have this target, try to do less than you thought you would on your travel run. You can always come back if you're interested in other things. The same thing, by the way, is with guided tours, for example. It's always funny to see when tourists run behind the travel guide with the red umbrella, believing this might have something to do with travel. It gives you an overview of some historic places or buildings, but it doesn't replace going out there on your own. So how would you plan such a trip, for example, to Paris, France? I'll show you:

- Planning activities is always an arrangement between time, money, and interest. You have to think of it as an accountant: How to maximize your investment so that everything suits everyone in your group. And still, believe that less is better than too much. So when you're visiting a city, I would suggest a centrally located hotel. That saves you time traveling around the area and leaves more time for the fun stuff. In our fictional Paris example, I would search for a hotel in the mid-price range in the Montmartre area. It's accessible on foot, has good public transport and taxis are nearby in case of rain. So now you've got the hotel booked, let's say for three days, let's start with the planning.

- The first thing on your list, no matter how stupid it seems, is the stuff to which your heart belongs. If you always wanted to see the Eiffel tower, don't plan anything else until you've made it there. That's your guiding light—your wish. If you have too many things in mind that you want to see, break them down into smaller destinations. Maybe you can squeeze something in somewhere later, but don't get fixed on that. Dreams and heart come first, the rest later on. My advice would be, don't include more than two tourist sites in one day. The reason is that often you have to wait in line, especially if you're traveling to famous buildings or constructions. There is always someone waiting, believe me. This will cost you time and stress you out if your list is packed to the roof with stuff. So only leave the two items you absolutely want to visit on the list. The cool thing is that if you should be unexpectedly faster, you just add one of the things from the next day to your list. This will give you a good structure and help you cover the things you're actually there for. So, do you have your two items on the list? Great, let's take another step. Ideally, you should choose two attractions that are close together, optimizing time and avoiding wasted traveling within the city. And maybe you can even walk between the two and smell a small pie of the non-tourist action in the process.

- Now check out online tickets to your attractions; maybe it's cheaper when you book in advance. So now you have your hotel and the tickets for the things you want to see (and are already organized) in the same areas if possible. Fantastic!

- The next thing you want to do is think about food. How do you organize your day with a meal plan? I suggest having a big breakfast, skipping lunch, or having a small sandwich or similar. It saves you more space for the amazing dinners they have. You'll get breakfast in the hotel or close to it down the road, for sure! I always try at least one local restaurant for dinner. I feel bad when I see people visiting the most unique places on earth, and they just go to a burger joint from a fast food chain, where the food tastes the same as at home. So for dinner, you're absolutely open to suggestions. A good idea is to ask the reception guys or the concierge in your hotel for restaurant ideas. Tell them you want a place they would go to, not a tourist place. You would be amazed at how great you can eat for less money if you knew where to ask.

- Again, my last point in this chapter is to try the local things, especially in a big city. You can research before you arrive and get a feeling for the city you will be visiting. Every city has its own hidden groove you have to find. Mostly I start with street markets. Why do I do that? It's easy because I can see the authentic life of the people in the area. You can buy local stuff like food or other things you can use. And it brings you closer to culture, people and an understanding of the country you're in.

- I always think *collecting memories* should be your target—knowledge of the tourist stuff you've seen. I know a few will disagree with me, especially the ones who have ten days of vacation and think they may rule the world. I know that many people also do guided tours. There is nothing against them, and they definitely have their space in the travel industry. In my view, they usually try to push you through many things in the hope that you return and spend more money. I must say that during the last few years, I have also used a small local guided tour business, and I really love them. They are hosted by locals who are proud to live there and try to show you a good mix of culture, history, local life, and much more. They also might be a lot cheaper than regular tours organized by the major players in the market.

I hope that these points gave you some ideas for your next trip. Of course, this example is valid for city trips, beach holidays, hiking adventures, and even cruises. There is always a way to get close to real traveling instead of just being there and running away again. I am sure in the age of the Internet; everyone can plan a perfect trip. It just costs research time and ideas in advance. Whatever you can do before you leave for your destination, do it. It will save you money, nerves, and sometimes frustration.

What you can do when you're at your destination is to ask for advice at the local tourist information center. They are usually very good, and sometimes they offer, for example, a dinner with locals or other similar ideas. I can recommend that, and I think the world would be much better when people realize there is more out there than just the obvious tourist attractions. Travel means understanding, learning, and sometimes being shaken up by reality. You will never find a perfect spot on earth, I've searched for over 30 years already, and even in the Caribbean, it rains sometimes. But you will find happiness when you start to understand others.

Chapter 11:

A Word About Climates

and Seasons

Don't underestimate climate and weather seasons. I did this a lot in my younger years of traveling and learned really quickly that nature always wins and that humans are only a guest of nature's will. You have to understand that the climate, weather, and seasons can enormously impact our travel behavior. It would be best if you noted that when you plan a vacation somewhere out of your home base area. What do I mean by this? Let me start with an example.

Let's take a look at our good old Paris again. You're planning, with the love of your life, a romantic vacation hideaway in Paris. So you would wish, of course, to get the full Monty. Lovely walk along the River Seine, sitting outside with a good glass of your beloved French red wine and enjoying the scenery. Let me say this nicely: When you're sitting outside in Paris during winter months, you could freeze to death and take the red wine with you. Europe in winter is pretty cold; I mean snowy, windy, humid, nasty cold. So think about if you want to go to Europe in winter, even if it's warm where you live. Another classic example is Australia and New Zealand. These countries are south of the equator, which means they have the opposite season from yours, living north of the equator. And so it goes on and on. Let me give you a short list of advice about how to find out if it's good to go there:

- If you want to travel to Europe, do it between May and late October. It's the typical summer season, and the chances of getting good and dry weather are the best. Southern Europe is warmer and more stable when it comes to rain. I would exclude the UK, Scotland, and Ireland for this tip. The weather in these countries is influenced by the Gulfstream and is usually wet, humid, and not very warm. You might think that Iceland is always very cold the whole year. But funnily enough, I went there once in January, and it was warmer than my hometown of Basel in Switzerland, which is much further south.

- If you travel to Asia, you can expect lots of hot weather, and even the nights are hot. Especially in Singapore, there is extreme humidity because it is on the equator. So when you travel during winter, Southeast Asia, with countries like Thailand, Malaysia, and Indonesia, is a safe bet. They usually have a rainy season, but I've traveled many times over there and must say, you can be fortunate and save a lot of money as it is off-season and the hotel prices are low. I personally would also give it a shot. One warning I have to alert you to is for Japan during winter. You can expect the same weather as more or less in Europe, so don't expect a beach vacation in Japan during January. Well, send me pictures if you do!

- Traveling during all seasons is possible in the United States. The country is so big that you can easily have warm locations, for example, in Hawaii, Florida, or California, even during the winter months. I suggest not flying via the Midwest during winter—cities like Chicago, Detroit, or others on the East Coast. The chances of blizzards (snow storms from the north) are high, resulting in canceled or delayed flights. I try to fly via Miami, Atlanta, Tampa, or Dallas when I have to change flights.

- The Caribbean is a safe place; the hurricane season during the summer months can be a problem, but usually not too much of an issue.

- South America is available throughout the year and offers lots of cold mountains and warm beaches. Also, the Amazon is a very attractive travel destination for the whole year if you like natural life and an adventurous trip.

- Many people don't realize that, for example, Seychelles or even Mauritius look the same as the Caribbean. But these islands are located in the Indian Ocean, not the Atlantic Ocean. This can confuse a few people, but I found that all seasons are great for these islands, and I have not had any issues at all.

So, when you want to travel, make sure you research on the Internet about the weather and what it's like at the time you wish to visit. It saves a lot of headaches knowing whether you will be freezing in a snowstorm. We spoke about flights, and this, of course, should include cruises too. You might have the answer when you ask yourself why a Mediterranean cruise is so cheap in November. The waves may be choppy, it could be windy and rainy, and it is questionable if you'd enjoy Santorini at 50°F (about 10°C) as much as you would during summer months with a beer in your hand.

Clothing is another thing you have to think about. When traveling to Singapore, you needn't bring your ski suit, as you won't need it. Always pack only as much as you need, but pack wisely. So you don't have to carry too much in your bags, and you might have more space for gifts or other related things you might buy during your trip.

So before you leave home:

- Check the weather at your destination on the Internet to get a feel for it.

- Pack the right clothes and shoes.

- If you go to warm countries, don't forget to bring sunblock (and a lot of it).

- Think about rearranging your travel if you see that the weather will be bad.

- Search for flights where you can be more or less sure you won't struggle when switching planes somewhere with bad weather conditions.

- Winter weather doesn't mean you will have a lousy holiday. The Alps, for example, is a great winter destination; just make sure you are prepared for the cold and snow.

- If you're a cruise enthusiast, make sure where you can make the most out of your cruise, and don't book something just because it's cheap. After all, it's your vacation.

Chapter 12:

How to Pack the Stuff You Really Need and Leave the Rest at Home

When I see what people pack to go for a trip somewhere, I often ask myself if they ever plan to return home again. You see mountains of clothes, a hundred pairs of shoes, and a bag alone for hairspray and toiletries. Ask yourself, how much of it do you really need, and what will you use on your trip? What I always do is count the days that I am away from home. Once you have this number, it is easier to plan how much you need to pack.

You can calculate, for example, that you will need a pair of jeans every two days—depending, of course, on where you are going. At least it gives you a point to calculate what to pack. Do the calculation with all your clothes and shoes and ask yourself if you really need them. You'll be amazed how much less you will pack. My tip with clothes is always to pack one piece more of everything that you need. This will be your emergency fallback plan if you, for example, spill drinks over it or similar. So you'll be on the safe side for sure. Also, think about where you are traveling to. Is it a warm destination? Then you'll probably need fewer clothes than going to the North Pole. When you fly somewhere long haul or transatlantic, I will pack another warm jacket if you haven't already packed one. Why is this? It hardly ever happens, but if your plane has to land because of an emergency, you make sure that you are prepared for it, even if it is in Greenland or Iceland. It sounds stupid, but it helped me once, and I was happy to be the one who did not freeze.

When it comes to medications, always take enough with you. It might be the case that you can easily buy painkillers or eye drops in foreign countries, and mostly, it's the same stuff everywhere. But if you take tablets from your doctor (prescription medication), pack more than you need—just for safety's sake. Also, when traveling to tropical countries, don't forget to pack some good sprays to keep mosquitoes and other blood-sucking insects at bay. They might be hard to get when you arrive at your destination. I always say pack smart, which means less is more. Also, packing more stuff can get expensive nowadays, especially if you travel by plane. When you travel a long distance, one bag is *normally, but not always,* included in your airfare. This means if you pack more than one bag, you have to pay a special transportation fee for this bag. And let me tell you, this really can get expensive! So you probably want to think twice if you need a kitchen aid and a hairdryer in your bag. If it comes to handbags and hand luggage, there are some extra things to think about.

Hand luggage is usually limited to 8 kg (17.6 pounds), and you may only take one with you on the plane. This prevents all passengers from bringing all their camping gear into the airplane's cabin. When you pack your hand luggage, be smart and logical in your packing mode. What does that mean?

- Pack belongings like power banks etc., first and on the bottom of the bag. You probably won't need them during your trip; they are best stored far down. All stuff that is heavy and not easy to break should go as far down as possible.

- If you pack tablets and laptops, ensure they are easily accessible because you have to pull them out at the airport security. The same goes for liquids and medications you want to take into the plane cabin. Ensure the liquids don't exceed 100ml; otherwise, the airport security will confiscate them. If you really don't need them, put them in the bags you check in.

- If you have dangerous goods, check that you can carry them before you start your journey if this might create issues or if you need additional documents to prove that you can carry them.

- Travel documents always belong in hand luggage and should be easily accessible. You will need to show your passport and boarding passes a few times before you finally take your seat on the plane.

If we speak about baggage and luggage, we should also discuss what to wear during your trip. What does this have to do with packing bags? It's simple: the clothes you wear during your journey must also be transported back. Especially if you fly during winter and your jacket weighs a ton and needs a lot of space in the bag, you have to calculate.

I try to wear clothes that are suitable for most eventualities. Let's say I am flying from the United States to Asia in winter. If you live on the East Coast, you'll need a warm jacket because it might be freezing. But you must remember that it's hot, humid, and sticky when you arrive in Asia. So you can pack an extra shirt in your handbag and change it during the flight. I do that pretty often. I have long jeans, which are also okay for the whole trip. But mid-flight, I would change my long shirt into a regular t-shirt. You can wear a hoodie for the rest of your flight, and you're prepared. You can easily remove the hoodie when you arrive and only wear the t-shirt.

Going in the other direction, you would do vice versa with the procedure. Make sure you don't get dressed too warmly on the plane; otherwise, you'll freeze when you arrive in the cold country.

When it comes to shoes, everyone has their own technique. I prefer sneakers, for example, to travel wherever I go. The reason for me is that I easily take them on and off in narrow airline aisles. I use them when going to the restroom and wandering around. You can also use the socks the airline provides you, but I've had the experience that sometimes people drop liquids on the floor, and then your socks get wet, and your feet freeze.

So we have spoken about what to pack and what not. When it comes to the bags themselves, I would advise the following:

- Make sure your travel bags are as light as possible but also as strong as possible. Airlines usually have a weight limitation for the bags; if they are too heavy, you'll have to pay extra fees. So, the lighter your bag is, the more stuff you can put in.

- You might think about a backpack if you're not staying in one place and have to walk a lot. They are convenient and easy to transport. Make sure you use the same logic we've discussed for hand luggage. The heavy things are packed at the bottom, and the lighter stuff is on top. Make sure you use a waterproof backpack or have a rain cover available. There is nothing worse than a soaking wet backpack.

Suppose you travel with special equipment like golf bags, surfboards, winter sports tools, or similar. In that case, I highly recommend checking with the airline before your check-in to ensure that the plane has the space for it. Transporting all these things will cost extra—for sure.

Chapter 13:

A Word About Money and Credit Cards

That you would need money on your journeys should be clear to everyone, of course! The amount depends on how much you're willing or have available to spend, but a few things always stay the same, no matter how much money you have for your trip. One big thing you will need is a credit card. Without a credit card, it's almost impossible to make reservations for flight tickets, car rentals, hotel rooms, and even trains sometimes.

In fact, credit cards make our life a bit easier—if they are handled correctly. I highly recommend setting a budget and a plan for what you will use your card for. It is easy to spend more money than you would like to if you don't have an accounting plan for yourself. I know that my friends in the United States might see this differently, but for me, the saying, "Don't spend what you don't earn," is still a good one.

Regarding travel, work smart and find out if your credit card company has an agreement with hotels, car rentals, or even better airlines. The big advantage is that you can pay for your airline ticket with a credit card. When you do that, you may collect some miles or points because you used your card. So, in fact, you have a win-win situation, and to be honest, you have to pay the price anyway.

I have two different cards, as I found out during the years of traveling that sometimes one card is more in use within a country than others. And by having two of them, I minimize the risk that I cannot use the card to pay for something because that card is not accepted. Also, the cards sometimes include insurance for canceled flights or similar—you should check with your card company. When you travel abroad, also find out about the extra charges for using it in a foreign country. Depending on that, you can use it or switch to the good old-fashioned paper money.

Speaking of paper money, even though we are in the digital age, it still definitely makes sense to change money into local currency. Sometimes, you'll find a few locations where credit cards aren't accepted, especially when you're hiking with a backpack into the wild. This situation also often occurs in Asia, where locals only take paper money. Make sure that you don't have too much paper money, though. Sometimes the currency rates are bad when you want to change the local cash back into your own currency, and you'll lose a lot of money.

There are other things you need to keep in mind. It can create difficulties to have a lot of cash on yourself. Because the thing is, if it gets lost or, even worse, stolen, you'll have nothing left. You can call the bank to issue a new card with a credit card, but paper money? If it's gone, it's gone.

I also suggest you learn about currency regulations when changing money. You are not allowed to export some currencies. This means that some countries, for example, Myanmar, do not allow the export of their currency. So you have to change your money back, at the latest, at the airport when you leave the country. Because the currency exchange agency at the airport knows that you have to do that, they might give you a pretty bad exchange rate. For this reason, ensure you only have as much money as you need for your stay. What usually helps is to change money in one of the major currencies, for example, the US dollar, Euro, or Swiss franc. Especially in Africa and Asia, you would be amazed how far you go by paying in US dollars, for example.

During your travels, make sure that the money is safely stored and not accessible for somebody to steal it easily. Also, *never*, I repeat, *never* pack your paper money into the baggage that goes via check-in into the plane. It will be out of sight; you won't be able to prevent someone from opening your luggage and taking the money. It also is wise not to place all cash in the same place but to split it up—if one part is gone, the chances are big that the rest is still there. And in hotel rooms, use the safe; that's what they are there for. If you don't have a hotel room safe, ask reception if they offer a secure storage option. This is still better than running around with tons of money on your body, trying to hide it from the world.

Chapter 14:

Understand the Geography

The world's geography can be confusing, complicated, and sometimes even weird. But when you travel, at least for me, it is part of the job to know where you are going. There is nothing worse than traveling somewhere unprepared. This includes the languages spoken at your destination and, as mentioned in the title, the geography. If you're visiting a city, this might not affect you as much as traveling around the country.

A good example is my home country Switzerland. You could visit my city Basel on one sunny and warm day, sit on a train and within an hour you'll feel the snow under your shoes in the snowy Alps. So when you come here to visit, you have to take warm clothes for the mountains and in summer your swimsuit if you want to jump into the river Rhein for a swim. So it would be best if you familiarize yourself with the geography of the Alps. Knowing there are huge mountains, you can plan precisely what you need to bring. This is an example, but when I travel, I usually check out a map and get a feeling of what to expect there.

It's, in fact, also fun strolling along routes and ways in your mind. And even if you're not good at geography, you'll get better and better the more you see the world. Geography is also taught by the Navy SEALs, as they say, "Know the terrain of where you are acting." Also, it is an advantage to know the geography and maps of the country as it will assist you in finding a way to travel around. It will not make much sense to look for a train journey in the Amazon jungle because it's a jungle—but you have to find out first.

If you don't like geography, make it seem like a game. The best way to practice is to look for transport availability and options. I do that sometimes for fun. Let's say I want to travel from Zurich in Switzerland to Orlando in Florida. How do you get there cheaply and fast? What is the weather when I will arrive on my pretend trip? Are there mountains or jungles? How to get around? All this helps you train for traveling, and believe me; sometimes the most stupid ideas show success too. Once, I had to change planes in Iceland in December when flying to New York. And guess what? It worked out well and saved me a lot of money. But I know Iceland is within the Gulfstream, a warm water ocean current. So Iceland in the winter should not be that bad, and it wasn't.

All these tiny puzzle pieces can finally make a big difference while traveling. And sometimes, these odd places you discover researching geography make it onto your bucket list—just for fun. One city I might have missed if it hadn't been for geographic fun is Utqiagvik, formally known as Barrow in Alaska. There might be nothing there, but I want to see the most northern city in the United States—just so I can see it. And this makes me, and maybe you also, a travel geek. But you know what, we love it, for sure!

The last thought I want to share is about the world's different seas. When planning a beach vacation, check out if the sea water is as warm as you expect it to be. When you're in Los Angeles, you might be tempted to hop into the Pacific Ocean. Do you know what I mean? It's very cold, even on sunny hot days, and it stays that way. The Gulf of Mexico, for example, will be different because the water is always a nice and warm temperature. I also always do some weather checks in advance and check how warm the water will be when you arrive. That gives you an idea of what to expect at the destination.

If you are more of a hiking guy, remember the higher you climb during your hikes, the colder it will get. You can freeze to death at high altitudes, even on hot summer days. Also, altitude sickness can be a problem. Walk slowly, and return when you realize you're not feeling well. It's always better to return home than to never return because of pride or other stupid things.

You may have to travel slowly in snow and ice, and you might need more time for your planned trip than expected. I always plan double travel time during the winter months, when the temperatures drop below zero degrees, to ensure I arrive safely at my destinations. Trains, planes, and other public transport can be impacted by ice and snow, and you might not get to your destination in time. Keep this in mind while traveling!

Chapter 7

A Word About Security and

How to Avoid Danger

Chapter 15:

A Word About Security and

How to Avoid Danger

Sadly, we have to cover the issue of crime too, because, unfortunately, our world has become increasingly unsafe. When you hear the news on TV or read the newspaper, you feel that the world's end is near. Lucky for us, that is just one side of the coin. The other one is that there are amazing people and places to visit. So don't let the fear win, but keep your eyes open. After traveling for so many years, I think I have a good eye for dangerous situations and things to avoid. I wrote a list about security for myself, and this is it. I recommend you keep an eye out for these things on your journey.

- When you're in a hotel, you are mostly very safe. But always lock the door, and if there is an extra lock, use that too. Sometimes there is also a chain to secure the door too. Ensure that the windows are closed properly, but most hotels today have installed windows you cannot open because of the air conditioning.

- When you rent a car, ensure you get a car where you can lock all doors automatically. This might be a little button that you can push while driving. When you do this, no one can enter the car, as it's locked and could be helpful at a red traffic light or an intersection. When you visit a tourist attraction or go shopping at some malls, always take a quick look at the backseat to ensure no one is hiding there. This might sound stupid, but during the 90s, this was a very common way to rob tourists. Always try to park close to the main entrance of your hotel. The closer, the safer you are because it's likely that many people are walking around. When you should drive around and feel stalked by another car, don't panic. Just continue driving and dial the number for the police. Emergency numbers should be part of the travel list you take with you.

- When you visit cities, avoid going into *bad neighborhoods*. If you're not sure, ask the receptionist in your hotel. They usually know because they are locals and live there. Go with your gut, I would say. If you feel unsafe, don't do it. Your mind is a better judge than you think and is always on the alert for danger. Trust your gut and your mind. Sometimes it makes sense to hire a local guide for some tours because they know the area, and also they know where it is safe to visit and where it isn't.

- On a cruise, I usually make the trips on my own because cruise excursions are pretty much overpriced. But if there are countries that are not so safe, for example, South America, then I suggest you book a tour through the cruise company. It's always large groups with many tour guides, which should help a lot.

- Pickpockets are like a disease around the world. They usually go for the easiest target, which means they want the quickest way to your wallet and your money. Don't take too much paper money with you, and trust cards because they are easy to replace. Always stash your cash in different places. So you ensure the risk of getting all your money stolen simultaneously isn't so high. Pay special attention when you ride a subway, use a train, or walk in dense crowds because that's the pickpocket's haunt. When using an ATM during your travels, ask a friend to stand behind you to ensure that no one sees the code or, even worse, snatches your money as it comes out of the ATM.

Finally, don't get paranoid, and enjoy your journey. Just keep an eye out; that should be enough to avoid the worst. There are more bright places than dark places to discover in the world.

Chapter 16:

How to Stay Flexible

During Difficult Times

This chapter is essential to me, and you want to know why? Because every traveler will meet this kind of situation. Whether it involves missing your flight, your taxi not arriving, or a very rude hotel receptionist—there will be difficult moments. The question is always, how do you deal with it? Our brain is trained to react to stress in different ways. Your voice might get louder, your nerves go crazy, and you lose control over achieving the main goal—to solve the issue that popped up now.

It took me years to understand that freaking out does not help at all. But how do you deal with this kind of thing? Start with finding out if it's something based on nature, for example, a thunderstorm, snow blizzard, or similar. It's nature, so when you cannot travel on time, nature wins. It's that simple. Say to yourself, "Okay, it is as it is. Let's see what happens when the storm is over and proceed."

On the other hand, there are many other situations you may have to deal with, especially when mother nature is not involved. These days, for example, plane schedules are switched in minutes. When you arrive at the check-in, the situation differs from what you expected. Please don't panic and be kind to the staff, as they always try their best. There are a few things that can happen during your air travel. If your bags don't arrive—then go to lost and found. If the travel itinerary changes, they will rebook your flight or let you know when the plane leaves. And finally, they cannot find your reservation. But even then, they will find a way, so save your nerves.

Also, remember to keep a cool head if something happens during your trip. You may not have a physical worst-case scenario plan, but you can think your way through the crisis. Say you travel to Hawaii, and your car rental plan blows up. They don't have a reservation or any idea how to give you a car to rent because they are all taken. Action from you would be to say to yourself, "Okay, let's find out about other car rental companies." If this is unsuccessful, switch to public transport or find a driver. For me, it is always good to know that there is a solution, always. The more you get angry and nervous, the more your brain shuts down, and you cannot think of a solution. You will feel like you are in a tunnel, and it is pretty hard to get out of there.

Not only travel journeys itself can cause nerves. Sometimes it is also the people around you. The world hosts different cultures with different views on things. Because it is right for you, it's only sometimes suitable for others. A perfect example of this is Southeast Asia. We travelers from the Western world always want to push people to behave like we do—capitalist thoughts and behavior. But for Asians, in general, it is more important to be humble and kind to each other, and the respect of people is a big part of their daily being. When you, for example, yell at a receptionist in a Bangkok hotel, they might be smiling at you, but you're a loser in their eyes. You will never get close to them or even get treated well. They will only do the bare minimum and not more.

It is crucial to accept that the world is colorful and different—in a few countries, people run around like crazy, and in others, people seem lazy. That's okay too. I think this is an essential part of traveling—understanding other countries and people. Only with this knowledge will we make new friends and get another worldview. You can see it as a mirror and ask yourself, how would other countries see you and your country? Then you will understand that the truth might be somewhere in the middle of the ocean. Probably, all are right, and all are wrong. Difficult moments get handled best with a lot of humor. Especially when you're on vacation, don't let yourself get pulled down by these situations, as they happen to everyone at some point. And these adventures mean you have stories to tell your friends years later when you look back and remember how angry you were in this situation. This makes us human in a crazy world. And traveling strongly teaches us what is important in life. To work together and find solutions for problems that might appear out of the dark. So think about this chapter when you next miss your flight because of bad weather or other circumstances. There is always another you can take.

Chapter 17:

Mindset of a Professional

Traveler

When it comes to mindset, every person is more or less different. Every one of us handles situations and circumstances differently. But I assure you that you can train to have the mindset of a professional traveler. What do I mean by that? There are people in this world who travel from A to B. They have no clue what could happen during their trip or what they could do to make it more pleasant. This skill is a mindset you have to develop. When you know, for example, that you are about to embark on a long-haul journey, what should you think about before you leave? Could you get a business class upgrade with your miles, for example? Do they have a hotel room within the airport? If you have a layover between two flights of more than four hours, could you freshen up there? Discover the little things that no others can see.

This all starts when you plan your trip. Plot the whole journey in your mind and find out if there are any parts you could improve. This is not only for flights but for the entire trip. When it comes to ground transportation, what is the most convenient option? Is there a way of saving money? Public transport could be fast and efficient from the airport. All these things are worth a thought, and trying to make the most of it. I plan my trips by writing a little diary to check what I can optimize. Let's take our Paris example again and see how this would look.

- I plan my travel dates and ensure I always use the local time from the destination. Otherwise, you will sooner or later have chaos. If you travel eastbound, you must add hours; if you travel westbound, you must calculate minus hours. With smartphones, it's easy to find the time difference between your home and your destination.

- The next thing is to check the weather conditions to see what you can expect when you travel there. You may have to expect delays with transportation during snow or similar. Also, it gives you an idea of the clothes you'll have to pack in your bag.

- Now it's time to organize the transportation, for example, the flight. Always start with the flights and work all other puzzle parts around them. The reason is that the flights are often the most complex thing to book on your trip, and when you have them saved in the box, you can check with hotels and other arrangements.

- We've booked a direct flight with a reasonable fare because we travel during the week. I even upgraded my miles to business class because I figured it would be a redeye flight. Night flights are always more tiring no matter how you fly and how long. If you can, try to sleep as long as possible, and if you have the option to upgrade, do this on night flights; it's worth more than with daylight flights.

- So now the flights are okay, ask yourself, how do we get to the airport? If you go in your own car, the parking fees are usually ridiculously expensive, for nothing. If a neighbor or a family member has time, that would be cool, of course! Are there public options like a subway, bus, or train? No matter how you plan to get there, plan enough time; otherwise, you'll stress yourself to death. The next question is, how do you get from the destination you're flying into your hotel? Check if the hotel offers a complimentary shuttle; they do that sometimes. Otherwise, check out for a taxi or public transportation.

- I always book the hotel together with the ground transport question. It would not make sense to save money on a cheap hotel in the "desert of nowhere." You would spend all the saved money on transport getting there and around. So for that, find a good balance between the price, the location, and the transport. There are thousands of options always and at all prices. With hotel rooms, always ask yourself: How many hours will you spend in them? If you're going to a beach resort, it makes sense to take a great room, but if you go to Paris? You'll spend the whole day walking and exploring the city, and you are not in the room. It has to be clean and safe, and the curtains in the bedroom must close properly so you can sleep easily because of jet lag the first few days. With all these indications, I am sure you'll find an excellent hotel at a reasonable price. Maybe you also have a loyalty program, and you might get a room upgrade when you stay at one hotel chain. Never be shy to ask for it.

- Now you are in Paris, and the city is very big. You'll need to take the famous "Metro" or the bus. I always would visit the city's tourist homepage because usually, it's informative, and you can easily find out how to buy tickets for subways or buses. Most cities offer special tickets when you buy them for a week or at least a few days. You find this information at the ticket booth of the transportation company or in advance on different sites on the Internet. Just make sure you use an official provider and not some spooky tour guide who promises the cheapest tickets on the planet.

- You may want tickets to some tourist places, like the Eiffel Tower. It is a really, really good idea to book these tickets in advance and bring them with you printed. You never know if the cellphone or similar works. Paper is still king. If you book in advance, the chances are high that you will get a space on your preferred date. And sometimes it is cheaper to book in advance than directly at the ticket booth.

- Shows and musicals can be worth a visit. If you're not too fixed on what you want to see, there are sometimes lower prices when you ask on the performance day. If they realize that the show is not sold out, the ticket prices will go down, and you can get cheap tickets and very good seats. But if you want to see a particular show, book in advance. Big shows are usually sold out or close to sold out a long time before the performance date you have in mind.

- Restaurants can also get booked in advance. This makes sense when you are with a big crowd or if the restaurant specializes in something. In Paris, for example, you'll need a reservation to enjoy a not-too-expensive French kitchen with authentic flavors.

So you see how to puzzle the trip together. You'll find your own way of working, for sure! And this is only an example of how it can be done. It really matters where you are going and what cultural and weather conditions you'll find at this place. Stay flexible and never give up on figuring out a way that works for you. Travel is sometimes like collecting things until you're ready to rock.

Chapter 18:

Environment and Green

Planet

It might be clear to everyone that our planet is in danger. But also, to be realistic, there always will be travelers going from one point to another. Not only for fun but sometimes for business, to visit sick relatives, or other circumstances. It is easy to blame people for flying in general. But remind yourself that sometimes, flying is the only option you have. Especially if there are oceans between two points or the distance is too far to cover using other transportation. But, we must use flying resources carefully and wisely. It does not make sense to take a plane for a route you could travel to in a car in two hours or one hour by train. That's ecological nonsense. With that in mind, I made a little list: of how to take care of the environment and use more eco-friendly travel.

- When I use planes, I avoid flying routes in the wrong direction. What I mean is that sometimes flights are cheaper when you detour over the airline's home airport or at least a city that is not directly on your path to your final destination. So it would make little sense to fly from Los Angeles to Chicago and then fly to Hawaii because you could fly from Los Angeles directly into Hawaii.

- All these tips have additional costs but think about if you're willing to create more exhaust gasses than needed. Several years ago, airlines started an option for travelers to pay extra to compensate for the exhaust gasses produced by their travel.

- I would do everything within a three-hour travel radius using transportation other than flying. The reason is not only the environmental issues created by planes, but it's easy to see you save time getting to your destination. You might think three hours is quite a long time, but now consider what you must do if you take the plane. You cannot only calculate the actual flying time. You have to calculate starting from your house to the airport, check-in, security, going to the gate, waiting for boarding, actual flying time, waiting for bags, going through customs, and transport to your destination. In most cases, you would be faster with the car—especially if your flight is delayed or canceled.

- When you like going on cruises, you will know it as well. The cruise ships blast bad air into the atmosphere and don't care about the environment. But on the other hand, there is a sea change in attitude, and more and more ships are installing engines with gas turbines instead of dusty diesel. You can always check if there is a cruise you like with a gas engine instead of a diesel engine.

- When traveling in Asia, you will know that whatever you buy comes in plastic bags. The problem is that these countries often need to learn to recycle plastic correctly and not just discard it in the woods or landfills, where it is left to rot for the next few thousand years. Try to bring your own shopping bag, or let the seller know you take the goods under your arms. You will save a few bags and make the jungle cleaner.

- Meanwhile, eco-tourism is an excellent standard in the industry. Many hotels have also hopped on the train with this idea. You'll find many hotels labeled with special environment prices or similar. Also, consider if you need a bathroom towel service every day. Most of the time, a towel change every second day would be more than enough and saves water, soap, and electricity. If you research the Internet, you will find many eco-hotels that offer pretty much the same amenities as regular hotels but take great care of our green planet.

- When organizing tours, ensure they offer a greener version of the classic hop-on hop-off bus tours. In the most scenic landscapes, you won't find on tour buses or taxis. You have to walk there on foot to discover every corner of it and really feel that you are there now.

- Especially when you're taking a vacation in Europe, there are amazing opportunities to take a train, even when you visit more than one country. The advantages are that you see something from the scenery and life outside the window and do something for the environment. Almost all trains in Europe have electric engines and don't blow exhaust air into the world. Trains also offer great value for your money, and for the speed junkies, they travel pretty fast. They are efficient, and no one wants to take a plane when you can take a train and ride it at 180mph.

- Also, when you do car rentals, it is known that all the big players in the market also offer more or less good electric cars. Not many years ago, people may have yet to consider this, but these days there are more and more electric cars to choose from, and the prices are in the same range as any other midsize car you can rent. If you rent an e-car, make sure there are facilities to charge the battery while traveling; otherwise, you might have an issue during the trip. But I think it's an excellent opportunity to try something new and do something for the green footsteps of our earth. Sometimes the big car rentals offer these cars also with cheaper conditions, so don't hesitate to ask them about it.

Chapter 19:

Bucket List and How to

Not Become Disappointed

Bucket lists can be a curse in a traveler's life. Even if you can fulfill a complete list, new places you want to discover and explore will arise. I think it is crucial that you create realistic bucket lists. I mean, for example, that it might be difficult to visit a destination, and you will be disappointed because it will remain unmarked on your to-do list.

I know many people who make the bucket list in the order it comes to mind. But it makes more sense, if possible, that you sort them one way or another. You can do this as travel locations within a country, or you even can do it by including the targets in your travel plan. A lot of people have dreams about unique places on that planet. The issue is that you won't be the only one going there these days. In my childhood, you went somewhere, and you could be sure it was a place just like you imagined. Today? One picture on a social media platform with a girl in a bikini looking excited into the camera and this place will be jammed by tourists. If you ask me, I am unsure whether this is better than the old days or different. So expect in general, especially when you visit big monuments, that you won't be alone to enjoy it.

Hordes of tourist buses swarm around and make the destination on your bucket list look like a joke. To avoid this, you can try to check out the big tourist things shortly before they close or get there before they open. It sounds stupid, but for me, the Colosseum in Rome is always nicer when it rains because most tourists stay away. Unpleasant weather can be your friend for sure. Even ice and snow might be better sometimes than standing in a queue for three hours to see something.

Also, I found out that most tourists are lazy, which means if they have to walk to see something, only a few do it. One story I remember was when I visited Zion Canyon in Utah, United States. The national park has many parking lots where you can drive your car to the front of the attraction. But no one in the States seems to walk at all. They sat in their pick-ups, drinking soft drinks and having three burgers rather than taking a 10-minute walk to see the park's natural beauty! We saw only three walkers when there were around 20 cars parked looking at the site out of their vehicle windows. We went on a hike that lasted at least 30 minutes and took the most wonderful pictures without a single person around us. We even got a photograph with a coyote. Just amazing. We would never have seen all this sitting in an air-conditioned car. So going the extra mile is worth it if you really want to experience something. That's my experience! When you succeed in visiting the destination on your list, don't just take in the site, but celebrate it proudly and tell yourself, "Hey, I did that."

I think traveling is a masterclass of education anyway. You get confronted with many cultures, issues, and things you don't understand, and what do you achieve in the end? The magic of ticking that point on your bucket list.

Consider booking in advance if you have sporty things on your list, like bungee jumping or similar. Often you get better prices when you book a while before you want to do it. This saves you money on the one hand, and on the other, you finalize the last step before you do it. This feeling is also fantastic, to take action and to know, "Yeah, I am gonna do this for sure."

I think these kinds of lists show our inner wishes and explain why we are who we are. If you're an art lover, you want to see the world's greatest museums, and when you are a sailor, for example, there is nothing more special than making a transatlantic journey on a yacht. You can choose whatever you want to put on your list. The only point you need to be aware of is that you will be disappointed when you try to finish a list that doesn't come from your soul. *You* have to do it, and it's your dream! Never forget that when you plan a destination on your list. Ask yourself: Is it something you want to do from your inner core? If you are not 100 percent sure, put this destination at the bottom of the list and check later in life if you still want to do it.

Even lists can change when you get older. A few might want to see the North Pole, while others want to see the lake in the next city. Everything changes in life, even bucket lists. And the more you travel, the more you'll understand that life teaches you that nothing is permanent. I guess this was the hardest lesson I had to learn because I am not a huge fan of change. But life pushed me there, and it was not as bad as it seemed after a while. Life is about finding its way anyway if we like it or not. So you better go with it and find some unbelievable places on your great planet. And never forget, sometimes the greatest outdoor sites are just around the corner of your house. You just need time and the motivation to find and discover them for yourself. The bucket list is like your soul, finally. Luck is where your heart is, and there you should go to find it. Small things can bring you more joy than big ones; that's what I've learned so far in my life.

Chapter 20:

Get the Views, Feelings, and Understanding of Foreign Cultures

As we have already spoken a bit about, travelers need to know that it will be different from home. Even if you go to countries near home, you'll discover other cultures and traditions that differ from how things are at home. But to be honest, that is the reason we go traveling, correct? If everything would look the same, why go somewhere else? I think these days there is a new *hobby* for many people to make other countries look bad or backward. But always ask yourself, how do other countries see your country or yourself?

I always found that you are pretty welcome anywhere in the world when you go there with an open heart and a positive mind. Inform yourself before you travel what to expect at the destination. A few countries have different rules, and they stick to them whether you like them or not. You can expect, for example, to get no meat from pigs when you're touring through an Islamic country. Also, the alcohol will be hard to find or won't be available at all. But when are you aware of it in advance? Easy thing.

Also, remember that, especially in Asian countries, respect, and honor have a very high priority for the people. So try always to be respectful, even if a mistake or something unexpected arises. The more you shout or scream, the less you will become in Asian countries. You will lose face in their eyes, which is the worst thing. Try to find a solution politely, and you will find people will try everything to help you. This often has to do with their view of karma. They don't want to create negative karma. So you can expect good or even great service in Asia, but be kind and friendly to them. At least, a bit of respect should be an everyday thing, no matter where you are traveling.

Inform yourself about the country you are visiting and its people. When you arrive at a new destination, I recommend finding local guided tours; I have mentioned this earlier. This gives you a real view of their world and daily life struggles. And you will see much more than you would see just running around and doing the touristy stuff.

I also love being on cruises because it is such good food, value, and most of the time, an excellent way of traveling, and you only have to pack your bags once. The negative aspect is that with 90 percent of all cruises, you spend only a few hours in a port.

Usually, you arrive at a port in the morning, and in the late afternoon, the ship heads to the next island or port of interest— this makes it difficult to get an accurate view of the country or island I am visiting. Mostly the ports are made for tourists and have nothing to do with the country. You stumble out of the cruise ship and are immediately surrounded by cheap t-shirt shops or tax-free cigar shops. On the other hand, there are tours organized by the cruise company. The good thing about these is you are sure you will be back at your ship in time. The bad thing is that these tours mainly only cover tourist attractions and seldom show local things. You only get a very limited view of an island! Don't you think so, too?

What I do in advance when I think I could be interested in the culture of a place I am going to visit is I write the destination's board of tourism or I do some research to find out if there are local guides around to show me the real deal. Most of the time, they are even better and far cheaper than just sitting in an air-conditioned bus and waiting with hundreds of sweaty tourists for your ride.

My final message for this chapter is to keep your heart open to new places, new friends, and many things you might not understand from the beginning. I wish that people in this world would do that much more often. A lot of misunderstandings would be averted, and a better and more human life would be possible for all of us on this great and lovely planet earth.

Chapter 21:

The Difference Between Traveling and Just Being There

I think that this is a crucial topic. The problem these days is that most people go somewhere without getting the feel of travel. I know this isn't very clear, but let me explain it. You might know of one or another influencer, maybe. In the old days, we would say they had no formal employment. Today they are in front of the Egyptian pyramid in pink high heels staring into the sun armed with their cell phone camera. Do you think that these people really travel? I think these people are just there without knowing much about the place, the culture, or other things. And this is the thing. If you travel, you make plans in detail. You learn about the history, culture, food, and many other things that people who are just there will never understand. This also might be why backpack tourists see much more than people who hop into a plane and jet to one place.

Traveling should not only show that you can prove that you were at some specific location on earth. It should be the experience of a whole range of things. I always remember much more about little things than the big touristy places. My brain has captured more of the moments having red wine with strangers sitting on some stairs in Florence, Italy, than the monuments surrounding us. Travel should be about meeting people, meeting life, going home afterward, and understanding much more than you did before. And, I guess, this is the thing you should make clear for yourself. There is a difference between just being there and traveling. Don't misunderstand me; you can also take a beach vacation at a very touristy place and still travel instead of just being there. You could go where the locals hang out, organize a tour to places off the beaten footpaths, and be amazed at how many things are possible to visit.

Another thing I want to mention is the habit of taking photos of all and everything. Do you know this kind of guy who takes pictures of every ant they find during their travels? They collect far more pictures than most people on earth, but what do they show you? Very little. I really try to minimize taking photos for the following reasons. Let's be honest. How many times do you look at your pictures after you get home? I guess it's not so much as you think you will when you take the photos. It is not a race where the person with the most pictures wins something.

Swap quantity for quality, I would say! Do take a really beautiful picture of an amazing waterfall, but there is no need to take photos of the glass of water on the table at a gas station, so to speak. Because the thing is, the more pictures you take, the more you will be busy taking them physically. You might miss one or another situation because you were constantly fiddling around with the camera or your cell phone.

In my experience, this might limit your travel experience. I also take photos, but only if they are worth getting. And I might only have 20 pictures after my vacation, but these 20 pictures are close to my heart. I can be sure that I look at them more often than others who take over 1,000 pictures and walk around their destination without really seeing it. And as long as you know that you have been to all the places you wanted to go, you don't have to prove it to anybody else. Traveling is not about collecting the most pictures of tropical islands; it's to be able to reminisce with friends and ask, "Hey, you remember that little bar in Havana?"

Chapter 22:

Special Case: Traveling in

Europe

I've decided to say a few special words about traveling in Europe. When you are from the United States or Canada, or even generally from outside Europe, you'll find out a few things here that will be useful.

- Driving cars in Europe is expensive, no matter what country you choose. Gas prices are high, the cities are narrow, parking is sometimes almost impossible to find, and parking facilities are costly. Also, many European countries have high tolls for freeways or other roads.

- If you want to visit big cities, the best way is public transport, and most of the time it's cheaper, and could save you some nerves. The distances in Europe are smaller than in other countries, and it's wiser to take a train, public bus, or plane than to rent a car. You'll often find special fares if you book early.

- Hotels within the city centers can be very pricey too. Check out for a hotel outside the city center but very close to public transportation. That can be a city bus or a street tram. Sometimes you are within the city center in only five minutes with public transport, but you save tons of money because the hotel is cheaper out of prime locations.

- Europe and winter are not best friends. Don't fool yourself and expect Barcelona, for example, to have high temperatures during December. You can get lucky, but Europe is mostly cold, damp, wet, or even snowy from November until the end of April. I know many friends in Greece, for example, who still freeze at 40°F during March. Although you can plan a city trip in winter without worry, just be prepared for the cold weather and sometimes snow-related issues. Airports often struggle if there is snow and ice.

- Europe is split up into very different countries. Even when most of them are within the European Union zone, they have their history and country-specific things. Stay flexible with your travels, and don't wonder why a few countries seem well organized and others not so much. When you speak English, you might have no issues finding people who speak English too.

The European school system is good, and even kids learn English or other languages swiftly.

- If you are interested in seeing much of the Mediterranean Sea, I suggest doing a seven-day cruise. You might visit Rome, Naples, Cannes, Barcelona, and other exciting places and save money on the cruise ship. Even for beginners, a cruise is often a bargain instead of visiting all these places separately. You could do the same on rivers, for example. Many river cruises in Europe bring you to lovely places. You would not need to book separate trains or similar. The Rhein is an excellent river to travel, as is the Danube. Prices can go down depending on the time of year you want to visit. Also, the river cruises are flexible and sometimes offer Christmas shopping in different cities. It's cold then, but it also has its special charm.

You see, visiting Europe can open an entirely new view of things. Everything is a short distance for traveling, and you can see a lot. But also make sure that you not only race through the cities but become a part of it, as this is Europe.

Chapter 23:

Food Happiness Around

the World

Food belongs to travel just as waves belong to an ocean. Wherever you go, you will catch up with local food, more or less. It might be clever and wise to research what to expect in the country you visit. For example, when you visit India, you can expect to taste curries that might be very hot and spicy. It is always weird to find out that Italian food in Italy tastes completely different than when you would visit any Italian restaurant in the United States, for example. It's not only the ingredients themselves but the way the food is presented. Try, for example, to find spaghetti with meatballs in Italy; it's almost impossible, I would say!

Another important thing today about food and traveling is the health aspect. Many countries cook differently, and it might affect your health and your stomach. The travel quote, "Boil it, peel it, cook it, or forget it," still stands today. When you are on a street market in a jungle and see a stall with ice cream, ask yourself: Is it really safe? How do they make the ice cream here? It's just a matter of fact that the chances of getting sick are higher trying it out than staying away from it. The same goes for ice cubes—I have to warn you. Leave the ice alone if you are unsure where the water comes from and who produces the ice. Meanwhile, many restaurants write on their menu that their ice cubes are made from bottled water. Then you can be sure that you are safe and won't suffer because you added them to your drink.

With all these safety issues, don't get paranoid and over-cautious.

If you follow the basics and think for a moment before ordering, you will be absolutely okay. In fact, it is great to explore new food and local markets with local specialties. And believe me, the food you will enjoy the most is the more authentic cuisine from the country you're visiting than similar foods you buy in your home country. This is not only the location; local herbs, for example, are unavailable in your home country.

Trying out new food is the most fun part of traveling the world. It gives you a view into the soul of a country. Don't be shy about trying new things and get a new food horizon of your own. If you stroll around local markets with fruits, meats, and vegetables, you'll get a good indicator of how the people cook in that country. You could also take a cooking class from a local if you are interested in cooking. No one can show you more about local kitchens and cuisine than a local, of course! And it is a good chance to get a country's rhythm and vibes.

You can also visit local stores or markets to save a lot of money. The prices are mostly moderate, and the food is good. The trick is always to go where most people are standing in line. Do you know why? They already have had a good experience. Otherwise, they would not stand in queue and patiently wait their turn.

A last point to mention is airplane food on long-haul flights. I know many travelers are picky with the food on planes, but let's face it, you are only on the plane for a few hours, and once at the destination, you have all the time to enjoy a good restaurant. So, don't be too hard on them, even if we know that the quality is acceptable at most. I usually go for the vegetarian dish on long-distance flights because the meat is often kind of scary for me. And I stick to black tea with no sugar to stay hydrated. Coffee is mostly of poor quality and messes up your biorhythms because it contains caffeine. Also, plain water should keep you safe and hydrated till you arrive at your destination. If you don't trust airlines at all, you also could bring your own food, just keep in mind that it should be easy to handle in your handbag and that the smell is not too bad on the plane. To make a cheese fondue for yourself on a plane is not a good idea, so to speak!

Chapter 24:

Why Traveling Should Become a Part of Education in School

If you think about how the world changed during the last few years, it might be a good idea to teach some travel content about foreign cultures during school hours. It's not the travel that should get a place in school, but the meaning or understanding of different views on the world. I always noticed that it's easy to say that other cultures do this wrong or that wrong, but who decides what is right or wrong? Maybe people from different countries think the same about us people from Western countries, and they might feel that we are weird in some way too.

I learned a lot during my years of spending time visiting different places and traveling around the world. The most important part was always that no matter where you go, the problems and things that everyone has in common are the same things that concern you. It's about whether your kids are happy and healthy. It's about how to pay all monthly invoices and cover insurance for your family. We seem to be very different sometimes on this planet, but we are also very much the same; this is important to keep in mind when it comes to travel. Young people especially want to explore the world and see what's around the next corner. And the more they see, the more they experience what it means to learn about cultures, food, new friendships, and natural beauty they've never seen before.

Many readers might think that traveling is always about money and time. But ask yourself; it also could be a travel tour just to the next big city around you for a weekend. You would be amazed how much there is to see around you. I always believed in my younger days that the further a destination was away from home, the better it was. So, in fact, I thought that traveling becomes more fulfilling when you choose a destination that's at least as far as the back of the moon. After many years of running around, I realized a few of the greatest destinations are actually around the corner from where I live. But it took a while until I understood this.

So to finalize this chapter, if you are parents with kids and you get the chance to travel with them, do it; they will never forget it, for sure! Also, your local school may organize some exchange programs with other schools around you. This is a good way to experience brighter horizons away from home and discover new things.

Kids will learn to work with others in a team; they will learn new languages much quicker than in the regular class because they can use them in the country and so on. All this will strengthen today's kids and prepare them for our new global world. I also think that globalization will become even more critical in the future, and the world as we know it might feel smaller and more connected in any way.

Chapter 25:

Travel Documents and

How to Prepare Them

I know that this documentation is a pain, but a necessity. In fact, every traveler wants to travel quickly from A to B without carrying a bag full of papers. And yes, in the old days, meaning traveling about ten years ago, it felt easier than today. Depending on where you travel, you might need different documents. Let's take a complex travel example so that you know what to expect in the worst-case scenario.

Let's assume you plan a trip from destination A to destination B. Your destination B wants to have a visa for entry that you need to organize as well. How do we start?

- The first thing is to book your flights. If you have done that, print out your boarding pass, even if you have it on your smartphone, to make sure you have it available.

- Then check your passport and make sure that it's still valid. I always check that my passport is valid six months after returning home. So I stay out of trouble for sure. If you already have stamps in your passport from different countries, ensure they don't cause issues when you enter your travel destinations. Always good to research in advance if there are any travel restrictions.

- A visa is always one of the most annoying things you must get for several countries. There are two forms for visas. The first is called "visa on arrival," meaning you fly to your destination and pay the fee to immigration staff. After that, they will stamp your passport with the visa approval. Then you collect your bags, and that is it.

- It gets more complicated when you need a visa before you travel. So, usually, you must show it during check-in. You will also need to show your visa to the immigration officer at your destination. So how do you get a visa? As always, there are many ways to get them. Often you can go via a travel agent, and for a fee, they will get you the needed visa. If you book a guided tour, usually the company will take care of the visa. Another idea is to contact the embassy from the country you want to visit and ask what you must do. The worst case is when they insist you come in person to apply for and collect your visa. Some countries handle visas electronically, which is great, of course! No matter how you get your visa, it will take time to get it. The flight and visa are always the first things I do when I travel somewhere because you can easily add the rest in the end.

- When you book a hotel, you usually need an identity document or passport, and you'll have to present a credit card, which is easy.

- Car rentals are similar to hotel reservations. You can book online, and the car rental company will send through your confirmation number. Bring your credit card, passport, and, most importantly, your *driving license*. Make sure that you have an international driving license to avoid issues. Most countries also produce international driving licenses in English; just ask your local department of motor vehicles (DMV) for it.

- Don't forget your insurance and your travel insurance card, as they will want to check them at the destination to ensure you are covered should anything happen.

Chapter 26:

Illness During Your Travel

Journey

Sickness is never a pleasant thing, that's for sure. No matter if you're traveling or if you're at home, it's just annoying and unneeded. Depending on where you travel, you have only limited options to buy drugs or other needed things that you need. I usually pack as much as I need, but the less, the better. For example, it makes no sense to pack four bottles of eye drops when you are sure you will only need one. It's unnecessary weight on your backpack or your bag. It also matters if you travel to a destination with more or less infrastructure. When traveling from New York to Boston, you will need much fewer medical things than when you travel into a desert in Africa. Keep all this in mind, and you'll be fine. Here you'll find a list of things that should be in your first aid pack.

- One of the most common things that can happen during traveling is, for sure, diarrhea. It's not only bad food that can cause diarrhea but also stress, time zone change, and different weather conditions. The best advice is, for sure, to drink enough water or tea. There are several good drugs against it, and they belong to your first aid kit.

- Cold and flu tablets should also be part of your pack. Especially when you travel to hot countries, you easily catch a cold because of air-conditioned rooms, ice-cold planes, or weather-related changes. It makes sense to buy something that fights against all symptoms instead of taking tablets for each. Also, make sure it is for coughs and lower a high fever.

- Don't laugh, but nose spray and ear drops are essential, especially when flying. When your nose is blocked, it can be painful to fly because of the air pressure produced in the cabin. So your nose and ears have to stay open whenever possible.

- Plaster and bandages are also helpful. Don't take too much, but a few. When you pack plasters, I recommend packing a roll of adhesive tape. It is useful not only for medical issues but also for sealing shampoo bottles or similar.

- When you pack hardware, so to speak, I suggest that you have a little knife with you. A Swiss Army knife with many functions in one tool is the best. Also, a pair of scissors is for sure helpful. Tweezers can be helpful if you get a splinter or a bee sting.

- My expanded version of my first aid kit is for countries without a very good medical environment. Most of Africa and parts of Asia belong to that category. When I travel there, I make sure that I also add an injection kit with me with a small needle. This would be my plan B to ensure I have a clean needle for any medical emergency. Charcoal tablets help with food I am not used to eating and could create problems. And I would pack some water purification tablets you can buy at many stores to make them drinkable. Make sure you boil the water first for a few minutes, and use the tablets, just to be on the safe side. Never drink water if you don't know for sure where it comes from. Better safe than sorry afterward is always a good tip.

Epilogue

Dear Reader,

In this book, I could not list everything that makes travel a pleasure—it would need thousands of books to do so, and even those would not be sufficient. Here are the absolutely essential tips when planning a trip. You will also find that certain things may be different for you than for me. The more experience you gain on your travels, the more you will write your own travel book and perfect the procedures.

I wish you wonderful experiences with your travels and unforgettable moments—always remember to live the moments. Photos are good, but living is better.

If you liked this book, I would be delighted if you would visit me on my homepage, *www.gilleskroeger.com*. I would also appreciate a book review so that other readers have a reference point.

Many greetings,

Gilles Kroeger

Made in United States
North Haven, CT
02 February 2024

48252445R00075